Corona Kids

By

A. E. Celik & A. K. Celik

Illustrated by E. Ozen

Once upon a time, there lived two siblings, the Magnifico and the Princess.

The Magnifico and the Princess shared lot of things...They shared the same bedroom and socks.

They shared the same bathroom.

They shared the same toys,
books, and beyblades...

One day, Magnifico and the Princess learned that there would be no more going to school for them because of a new virus called "coronavirus" which makes people sick, and some people sicker.

SCHOOL
SCHOOL
SCHOOL
SCHOOL

The Magnifico was super duper
cuper happy as they don't have
to wake up early and wear
uniforms any longer.

But, at the same time, he was super duper cuper sad.

His soccer classes and games
were cancelled too.

The Princess, on the other hand was very upset because she could no longer play with her friends in the playground. The Magnifico asked their mom about why their schools were cancelled and people were no longer supposed to do play dates, carnivals,

and birthday parties for some time.

So, their mom started to explain.

She first showed them a curly worm and said "Look, kids, this is called a ribonucleic acid, a.k.a. RNA." Its surrounding cushy stuff is called "protein and fat" she said. "This is what a coronavirus looks like".

Rna & Protein
Pcorective
Fat

"But, what does this thing do?" asked the Princess. "The fat around it protects the RNA." said their mom.

Once someone sneezes on you,
that virus tries to find a way to
get inside your nose.

And then your throat and your lungs are filled with super small viruses such as this.

Because these coronavirus feed on your body's nutrition, it weakans your own body and takes control like a vicious parasite. But, if your body is not weak, it fights back and fights back real hard.

So, "If you eat your fruits and vegetables, and wash your hands, your body becomes stronger and wins the fight against this virus, like other viruses".

"Sooooo" their mom said "Because people sneeze...

...cough, and touch each other at school, they closed the schools to help slow the spread of these viruses and protect the kids and their teachers."

"Oh, I know. If we eat our fruits and veggies, the schools will be open again?" says the Princess with excitement. "Oh, no way! One more reason to eat those greeny weeny skinny veggies" said the Magnifico.

"Yes, that would help immensely!" said their mom. "Do you know what else would help?" asked mom. "Wearing a mask to cover your mouth and nose!"

Then, they gave a big big big bear hug to each other at their home knowing the coronavirus will pass soon.

The End
☺☺☺

www.ingramcontent.com/pod-product-compliance
Lightning Source LLC
Chambersburg PA
CBHW042123110726
48006CB00003B/747